the sappy introduction

In the early days of 1994, thousands of Atlantans began writing a book. They just didn't know it. That's when The Atlanta Journal-Constitution opened the Vent, its now enormously popular feature that bids you to call in, without leaving your name, and blow off steam, leave a gag line or offer a twisted bit of philosophy.

The Vent has been called the poor man's Internet — a sort of audio bathroom wall. As of the summer of 1995, the Vent had logged more than 100,000 calls, and we decided to compile the best of them into **The Vent: The Book.**

By the way, and of particular concern to our attorneys, the Vent assumes that people are calling in with original material. When we discover otherwise, we don't use it.

Who's responsible for this?

Joey Ledford, opener and closer of the Vent for The Atlanta Journal-Constitution, edited this book. Most of what's here once appeared in the paper, although some of it was killed by our censors. We can put it in the book, though, because we're Vent people and we've got guts.

Richard Halicks, one of two diabolical inventors of The Vent, designed and produced the book. The other inventor — indeed, the Ventriloquist himself — was **Hyde Post**. He apparently was in charge of this endeavor.

John Amoss, creator of the demonic Vent phone illustration, did the cover of the book and the illustrations on each title page.

Larry Wilkerson, excellent Kentuckian, copy edited the book.

Zen
Vent

I can't compare them.
Oranges are better than apples.

I've just finished reading the obituary page
and I've discovered that people are dying in
alphabetical order.

Time flies when you're in a coma.

Be nice to your kids. They'll choose your nursing home.

Every day, my thoughts are printed in the Vent.
But the strange thing is, I never call them in.

zen vent

I've gone to look for myself.
If I should return before I get back, keep me here.

If you want to stop the neighbor's dog from using
the bathroom in your yard, why don't you lock the
door to that bathroom or, better yet, install a pay toilet?
Dogs don't have pockets to carry change.

I've come to the realization that I am a lesbian trapped in a man's body.

With all these crazies coming out of the woodwork, I believe the safest place to be is in the woodwork.

I had my cake and now I am going to eat yours, too.

Everyone knows that the home key on your computer is the one you push to go back to Kansas.

Vent: An opening for air or gas or liquid to pass out of or into a confined space. Truer words have never been spoken.

I learned everything

I need to know

in kindergarten:

Scream until you get your way.

Why does Madam C, my psychic, need Caller ID?

Since I've given up golf and taken up bowling,
I haven't lost near as many balls.

A truckload of human toupees turned over on 285.
Police are combing the area.

I loaned a friend of mine $2,000 for plastic surgery.
He never paid me back. What can I do now?
I don't know what he looks like.

Yes, I had an affair with Rose Kennedy
and I can't hold it in any longer.

I'm very happy the KFC corporation decided
to refurbish the Big Chicken. I'm a little concerned,
however, that every time I drive by,
the eye seems to be following me.

I've been standing in front of the Big Chicken for
45 minutes, and it's true. It is watching some
cars go by. What's going on?

I don't think anyone has noticed,
but the Big Chicken had a stroke.
If you don't believe me, look at his right eye.

For those of you who think the Big Chicken is
watching cars: You're right.
He's looking for a new coupe.

zen vent

In the event of a nuclear hit on Atlanta,
we'll direct the decent Yankees to 85 North,
the decent Southerners to 75 South
and the indecent others to 285.

Southerners, we from the North may talk loud
and dress goofy, but we know that bed
has only one syllable.

Not only should we keep the carvings of Confederate generals on Stone Mountain, we ought to add Elvis.

Was the Civil War fought in black and white?

I'm watching SportSouth. Why am I hearing about Notre Dame? Notre Dame on SportSouth is hypocrisy and sacrilege.

zen vent

The other day, I bought two bags of potato chips, opened them up and poured one into the other, just so I would feel better about life.

I don't understand what's wrong with the Fulton County tag office. Why is it so backed up? Also, the Mary Worth comic strip is getting more psycho by the day.

If they put hidden land mines on the course,
it would make figure skating worth watching.

Land mines would not make figure skating
worth watching.
However, they would make golf more exciting.

Has anyone else noticed Diana Davis' ears?
I think she's a Romulan spy.

Like the lepers, I think they ought to send all of us
smokers to an island. Like, say, Hawaii.

To the person who stole my car in Roswell:
Please return it.

If you love reading the Vent,
you should see a psychiatrist.
By the way, *I'm* a psychiatrist,
and I love reading the Vent.

I think fast-food restaurants should serve burgers
in the morning, instead of that breakfast crap.

zen vent

I always drop at least one ice cube when
I get ice from the refrigerator.

When I drop an ice cube on the floor,
I just kick it under the refrigerator.
It will melt, and the heat from the motor
will evaporate it.

zen vent

When they ban guns, only
disgruntled postal workers will have them.

Whoever does the pictures for the Vent
has the best job in the world.

I ate Bambi last night, and it was good.

I remember around this time a long time ago.
The men were preparing to go hunting.

The more people I meet, the more I like my dog, Otis.

Is Monroe Drive named after Doug Monroe?

zen vent

Santa Claus, if you come during deer season,
Rudolph is mine.

Every day, full of hope and anticipation,
I read the obituary column, but Larry still ain't dead.

Everybody who calls the Vent is an idiot
— except me.

zen vent

I have an average computer.
My friend has a fancy computer with a mouse.
Another friend has a real fancy computer with a gerbil.

I wanted to double my recipe,
but I couldn't get my oven up to 750 degrees.

I got a computer for Christmas.
Now my cat wants to play with the mouse.

zen vent

If the spacecraft needs to become invisible,
all it needs to do is project the rear image to the front
and automatically it becomes invisible.

My friend is learning to read by way of the Vent,
but soon his mind is sure to be rotted by what
he can comprehend. I know because I learned to read
through the Vent and that was just six months ago
and my mind is halfway gone now.

zen vent

My uncle said he would come back after he died
and he did. He even took time to get
Shirley MacLaine's autograph.

I have a question, but I'll ask it another time.
You just be ready for it.

I got a date at the Waffle House, and she was a psycho.

I wish I could find

a way to keep the birds

out of my squirrel feeder.

Romancing
the
Vent

When I turn 40, I'm trading my
wife in for two 20-year-olds.

I'm the wife of the man turning 40.
Trust me, honey, you're not wired for two 20s.

To all of you virgins out there: Thanks for nothing.

Yes, it's me calling again on a Friday night.
As you can tell, I lead a full life.

My wife can't stand me when I'm drinking,
and I can't stand her when I'm not.

I personally think the sexiest thing on a man
is dishpan hands.

Last night, I dreamed I killed my husband by
whacking him over the head with my cast-iron skillet.
That won't hurt the skillet, will it?
I mean, I'll still be able to fry chicken in it, won't I?

Love is blind.
Marriage is an eye-opener.

My boyfriend thinks I'm his backup plan.
But he's about to lose his backup plan.

I recently met a stripper. Is Apricot a real name?

I think the sexual revolution is over, and sex lost.

Is anyone else out there in love with Judy Jetson?

My wife thinks I'm too nosy.
I know that because I read it in her diary.

Every time I see one of those Taster's Choice
commercials, the only thing I can think of is,
please, oh please, don't let them breed.

If your husband decides to give his ex-fiancee a pager,
what's going on?

Why is it that every time you meet a guy, he asks if
you have a Sega Genesis?
Is this what keeps a man at home?

Are there male ladybugs?

My boyfriend of two months said he loved me.
Should I have said something besides, "Really"?

40

I went to France and saw some French whores.
You know, they're nothing like the French whores
over here.

My boss was out of town yesterday and I did it
with my boyfriend on her desk.

Is anyone offended by the billboard in Marietta
that says, "Fertilize your yard, not your wife"
for a vasectomy clinic?

The billboard in Marietta could be worse.
It could say fertilize your lawn with your wife.

I tricked my girlfriend into marrying me.
I told her she was pregnant.

I used to think something was wrong with my sister,
who never got married. Now, after I have had
two marriages and two children,
I believe she was a genius.

I keep forgetting:
Am I the opposite sex or is my wife?

I'm very proud of myself.
I'm the first member of my family in three generations
to marry outside the family.

My girlfriend just got her copy of the Victoria's Secret catalog. If they'd put cartoons in that, I'd cancel my subscription to Playboy.

When you remarry your ex, it's kind of like going back to prison.

So what if all the geese do at the golf course
is eat and multiply?
That's all my wife does
and I have no plans to shoot her.

Why does the newspaper print photos of newlyweds?
Why not print pictures of the newly divorced?
Let's see what's available.

My wife's away on a trip.
I need someone to come catch these dishes.

I need to know how come the older a man gets,
the younger and skinnier his girlfriend must be.

To the three women from Midtown who were on the
third floor of the Clarkesville Bed & Breakfast:
I believe use of a gag or vocal self-control
would have been appropriate.
Other people don't want to hear you.

Why is it when you reach the age of 40,
everything takes twice as long to do
— except sex, of course.

Man's fantasy:
Debbie does Dallas.

Woman's fantasy:
Darryl does dishes.

Hello ladies, I'm getting a divorce.
My getting a divorce is like Michael Jordan
coming back to basketball.

I truly love my wife, but my girlfriend
keeps interrupting
my concentration.

The pollen problem is killing my love life.
My boyfriend told me he couldn't kiss me and breathe
at the same time, so I told him to keep on kissing me.

Believe me, all men are not created equal.
I know because I've been married twice.

My girlfriend is having what she thinks is a
secret rendezvous
the first Monday of every month.
So now I have one every Saturday.

The weaker sex is the stronger sex
because of the weakness
of the stronger sex for the weaker sex.

You could say she was the best housekeeper in town.
Everytime she got a divorce, she kept the house.

Doesn't my boyfriend know that the only reason
I'm with him is because I'm afraid
I can't do any better?

As I get older I've changed from
a romantic to a rheumatic.

I don't have a boyfriend.
I have someone else's boyfriend.

A redneck divorce is just like a tornado.
Either way, somebody's going to lose a trailer.

I have finally figured out the movie ratings:
In G-rated movies, the good guy gets the girl.
In R-rated movies, the bad guy gets the girl.
In X-rated movies, everyone gets the girl.

The
Inquiring
Vent

If we can send one man to the moon,
why can't we send all of them?

Anyone ever noticed that the killer doll in the
"Child's Play" movies looks just like Neil Young?

Do Cynthia Tucker and Tom Teepen
fax their articles from Mars?

Is it just me, or does Meat Loaf look exactly
like Rush Limbaugh in a wig?

the inquiring vent

When there is a plane crash and they say they can't
identify anybody until they have dental records:
How do they know who your dentist was?

With all the technology we have
— 150 to 500 TV stations —
why can't they come up with the technology
so that Channel 2 is Channel 2 on your cable box,
and Channel 5 is Channel 5?

Now that Eldrin Bell is gone, will Michael Jackson
be designing the next police chief's uniform too?

I'm not disappointed with Willie Nelson for smoking
a little dope or playing a little poker.
But what in the hell
was he doing driving a Mercedes?

Why hasn't someone come up with a better sound
for the fax machine when you send a fax?

Why do men carry the newspaper
to the bathroom with them?

If God is a woman, does he have PMS?

Next time you print the Vent, can you make it two-ply and fluffy so I can have some use for it?

Would Stone Mountain Park please establish a "No Redneck Zone" at the laser show so that people with an IQ above 70 can also enjoy the show?

What is life plus five years?

Why is it that seven out of 10 women
in Peachtree City are named Megan?

Is it me, or does Zell Miller sound like
Mr. Haney on "Green Acres"?

It's not shorts in general

that God doesn't like.

It's those pleated khakis.

He hates those.

I want to know why the government can spend
millions of dollars to put a man on the moon,
but won't spend one dime
to get those people off Gilligan's Island?

Do vegetarians eat animal crackers?

Have you ever wondered how many ants
you have killed in your lifetime just walking?

Isn't "city worker" an oxymoron?

Isn't it obvious by now that the more laws you make
against dogs,
the more crime you're going to have?

My boss has a broken nose.
Do you think I overreacted?

Will somebody please tell me how to explain
the time change to my dog?

If the Waffle House is open
24 hours a day,
365 days a year,
why do they have locks on the door?

Are there any families out there where
all the members still have the same last name?

My family all has the same last name,
but I promise you it's a gene pool
you don't want to jump into.

What would a Q-Tip look like if we had three ears?

If we had three ears, a Q-Tip would look somewhat like a Mercedes logo.

If we had three ears, no one would own a Mercedes, because who the heck would want a car with a Q-Tip as a hood ornament?

the inquiring vent

How much of "Little House on the Prairie" was real?

Why do women wear one bra and a pair of panties?

Why doesn't Porky Pig ever wear pants?

Porky Pig doesn't wear pants because
he doesn't have anything to hide.

If Noah had a brother

would his name

be Yeah?

Anyone know what an arm and a leg
are worth these days?

When they ship Styrofoam, what do they pack it in?

If pizza delivery is free,
why is it cheaper when you pick it up?

Why do the people on "The Price is Right"
look at their friends like they have all the prices?

Am I the only person who thinks Martha Stewart
is scary?

I was just wondering: Do people really call in with
brilliant comments and ideas
or do you guys make this stuff up?

Doesn't anybody think it's weird
that the two terrorists who bombed Oklahoma
were both named John Doe?

What would happen if a poisonous snake
bit his tongue?

How come when you go to pay a parking ticket,
there is nowhere to park?

Why is it that when I drink two cups
of coffee in the morning,
I end up going to the bathroom six times?

Don't you just hate those people who call your house
and try to get you to buy something
that ain't worth crap?

Why is it that people who snore
always fall asleep first?

79

**Traffic
Vent**

I read that most accidents happen
within 25 miles of home, so I moved.

My husband calls Atlanta a city
of Forrest Gumps riding around in expensive cars.

I would use my turn signals on Atlanta roads,
but I think Atlanta drivers
see it as a sign of weakness.

Is it really OK for a motorcycle cop
to write me a ticket for no seat belt?

Traffic wouldn't be so backed up
if people would get off at their exit ahead of time.

How come the drive-up teller machines
have directions in Braille?

traffic vent

Why doesn't the DOT just close all the interstates,
finish all the construction
and call us when they're ready?

It seems that my car has some sort of built-in device
that causes traffic lights to change
from green to red just as I approach them.

traffic vent

BMW stands for Big Money Wasted.

I'm a mechanic.
BMW stands for Bring Money With ya.

My husband says that BMW
stands for Belongs to My Wife.

I may be driving a beat-up old Honda,
but now that my turn signals are broken,
I can pretend I'm driving a BMW.

One of these days,

when you throw your cigarette

out the window, the car behind

you is going to blow up.

traffic vent

I know exactly how you feel about getting that ticket.
When I was pulled over,
I had to resist the urge to ask the cop,
"What's the matter? Couldn't you catch the others?"

I was stopped in the HOV lane.
I explained to the cop I thought it was for people
who owned two or more cars.

traffic vent

A poem to all Atlanta women:

You look just fine the way you are,

Stop putting on makeup while driving your car,

That rectangular mirror you keep out of place,

Is intended for safety, not to put on your face.

Why do MARTA police ride around in cars?
Shouldn't they take the bus or the train?

Am I paranoid, or is there really
some desire to conspire against innocent tires?
I'm talking about those 4-inch-thick metal
serial-killer pothole covers waiting in ambush.

Does anyone know if they are going to fix
the 3-foot dip before and after every bridge
on the top end Perimeter, or do they have the same
dip working that put it in there in the first place?

I wish somebody could tell me where all these shoes
come from. You can be driving on 285,
on a country road or wherever, and you see a shoe.
One shoe.

traffic vent

How come you never actually see people
putting those orange cones down on 85?

To the woman in front of me this morning with the
Mothers Against Drunk Driving bumper sticker:
I hope the Budweiser you were drinking was good.

traffic vent

Be careful driving on the Ronald Reagan Parkway.
Like its namesake, you may forget who you are
and where you're going.

Whatever lane you are in,
it will end in 500 feet.

traffic vent

I've come to learn that the only thing
a car phone is good for is reporting the accident
you had while you were using it.

So those guys digging in the road are fixing it!
I thought they were looking for something.
They dig here and don't find it,
so they go down the road and dig there.

I have a Grateful Dead sticker on my car
and the cops say this is probable cause to search it.
Does anyone else think this is ridiculous?

If they are going to search cars with Grateful Dead
stickers for drugs, they should investigate those
with "Don't blame me, I voted for Bush"
bumper stickers for tax evasion.

traffic vent

How many cows would you say
it takes to upholster a luxury sedan?

To the driver who commented
about all the sofas and chairs on Ga. 400:
I guess if you get stuck in traffic,
you can stop and take a rest.

When one applies for a driver's license these days,
do they check out the mobility
of the applicant's middle finger?

To the guy driving the wrecker on Northside Drive
the other day, thanks, but I already know I'm No. 1.

traffic vent

When you're driving home on 285,
and you're stuck in traffic,
it's a lot harder when the person behind you
is real ugly.

Atlanta is no longer the city too busy to hate.
At 40 mph on the interstate,
I've got plenty of time to sit around
and hate the DOT.

Retiree seeks position
as dummy for the HOV lane.

**Topical
Storm
Vent**

Let's release Izzy into space
for the Opening Ceremony.

I think they should name the gorilla
at the zoo Magilla.
I think they should name all gorillas Magilla.

The people who support the anti-gay ordinance
in Cobb County think "Deliverance" is a love story.

Somebody please explain the logic of the
Georgia Legislature that one day condemns
Georgia Public TV for airing "Tales of the City"
and on another day gives a standing ovation
to the state representative who showed a young child
a fake penis.

To the person who said,
"Please stop the Tomahawk Chop because
it makes us look like a bunch of yahoos."
Hey, we are a bunch of yahoos.

After seeing the fabulous extravagance
of the opening of the Barcelona Olympics,
I have to ask myself: They have all that,
and we have Izzy?

In this day of clear Pepsi, clear shampoo,
clear flavored water and clear toothpaste,
I can't wait until Levi's comes out with clear jeans.

Just one time, I'd like to see Mr. Toyota jump up
and bite Tom Parks in the butt.

Don't you think that if the Virgin Mary
was really in Rockdale County,
the Roman Catholic Church
would have bought Conyers by now?

I wish everybody would stop criticizing the Atlanta
Police Department. It's the best police force
drug money can buy.

I hope all the Super Bowl visitors played a few Georgia Lottery scratch-off tickets, so they could experience one more rip-off before they went home.

Curb the proliferation of bigots: Distribute condoms free in Cobb County.

Well, it's nice to see that ACOG is going to be arbiter
of what is visually acceptable in Atlanta.
I guess I can quit worrying about it.

The person who considers the gorilla a non-native
of Georgia obviously has not taken a good look
at our state Legislature.

To Tom Charron of Cobb County:
If a drug trafficker can get off with $200,000
and beat jail, how much does a first-class murder
in Cobb County cost?

The Cobb County Drug Task Force
will not be beat in price,
and they guarantee it.

iii

Isn't it interesting that Grady
is running out of money for emergency care,
but they sure have a beautiful entrance.
So when I'm rolled into Grady and I'm dead,
people will say: "Too bad she's dead,
but isn't the entrance she's going through beautiful?"

Cynthia Goode, mother of a 6-month-old child,
writing a book on child-rearing?
Tell her to try again when the child is 16.

Movie popcorn tastes terrible now that it's healthy.

If Freaknikers ask for directions to downtown Atlanta,
tell them to get on 285 till it dead-ends.

If they need a voice for Izzy, they might try
Tom Shane or the gentleman
who represents the Men's Wearhouse.

The only event that could prompt
a so-called hunter to need any of the banned guns
is an invasion of 6-foot-tall ducks.

If the Hawks move to the suburbs,
how will the panhandlers and the hustlers
get to the games to greet the crowds?

Could we please get a police chief this time
who knows where he lives?

After reading the glowing defense
of Coretta Scott King in Friday's Vent,
I only have one question.
Which one of her children called it in?

topical storm vent

I was just reading about rapper Tupac Shakur.
I think they call him Tupac because
he is four short of a six-pack.

Evander, please don't fight again.
We don't want you ending up like Muhammad Ali.

Thank God.
Finally, a front page without an O.J. Simpson story.

I'll tell you what you call the man
who used to be called Prince.
You call him weird. Extremely weird.

If Michael Jackson and Lisa Marie Presley
moved into Graceland,
they'd have to rename it "Disgraceland."

I hope that I shall never see,
another slain body on my TV.

Celebrity Watch:
Tom Murphy dining at Old Country Buffet.
He ate both the pork and the barrel.

I feel real safe in this city.
The mayor and the police chief crack down
on Freaknik, but you've got the police
on the drug dealers' payroll.

How did the Georgia Lottery get 573,000
Olympic tickets? Did Rebecca Paul run up
$10 million on her Visa card?

I was wondering about

the pay toilets.

After 15 minutes,

does the ejection seat go off?

The Dead Heads are complaining about the pollen.
It's hard to roll and it won't stay lit.

Maybe Glenn Burns could forecast each day
what color Monica Kaufman's hair will be tomorrow.

topical storm vent

Is Izzy going to sell?
His eyes look like he's stoned on LSD.
Red nose — does that mean he's alcoholic?
Mouth large enough to drive a MARTA bus through.
Blue body; generally when skin turns blue
it's a sign of loss of oxygen, even death perhaps.
He won't sell at our house.

Well, the Southern Baptist Convention
is back in town. I guess all the strip bars
will be packed again.

**Poly
Sigh
Vent**

poly sigh vent

A Republican is someone who tells you
you can't burn the flag,
can't have an abortion,
tells you what movies and TV shows
you can't watch,
what CDs you can't listen to
and then tells you
the government is intruding too much in our lives.

While Hillary Clinton was covering up Whitewater,
Slick Willie was under the covers with Gennifer Flowers.
We know where his moral compass was pointed.

Hillary Clinton could probably stand the heat
if she had ever been in the kitchen.

Bill in '96 and Hillary in 2000.
What are those? Parole dates?

poly sigh vent

Occasionally, we put a Democrat
in the White House to remind ourselves
why we don't put Democrats in the White House.

I sent a letter to the president and addressed him
by "Dear Mr. President." He responded
and addressed me by my first name.
Charming. Maybe I should add him to my
Friends and Family calling circle.

You know what I hate

about political jokes?

They keep getting elected.

You're right, Mr. President,
there are plenty of great jobs here in Atlanta.
Would you like fries with that?

Is Bill Clinton going to stick around
for this weekend's Pot Festival?
Maybe he can get this inhaling thing right this time.

So the Republicans won.
Does that mean it's OK to be a white guy again?

To correct the person who vented about reptiles
and Newt Gingrich: Newts are not reptiles.
They are amphibians, which more appropriately
describes Newt Gingrich. They are cold-blooded,
slimy and a much lower form of life.

poly sigh vent

According to the latest economic reports,
"Don't blame me, I voted for Bush"
must mean I enjoyed having my family's net worth
reduced by $5,000.

If everybody who has a bumper sticker that says
"I voted for Bush" voted for Bush,
Bush would still be in office.

Don't blame me. I voted for Nixon.

poly sigh vent

I just invented a new gun designed especially for liberals.
I call it the affirmative action assault weapon
— it doesn't work and you can't fire it.

Flaming liberals should be extinguished.

The Republican Right should be called
the Republican Reich.

Newt is the greatest thing this country has had
since the invention of Brown Mule chewing tobacco.

Is Paul Coverdell related to Frazier's brother, Niles?

As a conservative white male,
I hereby take all the blame for what is wrong
with the United States.

If pro is the opposite of con,

what is the opposite

of progress?

**Psycho
Vent**

That's a man on the Quaker oatmeal box?
I always thought it was Barbara Bush.

If God is my co-pilot, can I drive in the HOV lane?

Did you ever get the feeling you're raising
the kind of kids you don't want yours to play with?

psycho vent

Now that Disney has bought ABC,
does that mean the network will be called ABCD?

I may or may not have a problem
with being indecisive.

My wife threatened to cut me off
and I said, "How can you?
You don't even know where I'm getting it."

psycho vent

There is a talk column called "Vent"
To which all our troubles are sent,
We fume and we spout
And bawl everyone out
And no one knows by whom it was sent!

If Hugh Grant and Charlie Sheen have to pay
for sex, I don't stand a chance.

Guns don't kill people;

bullets kill people.

Guns just make the bullets

go really, really fast.

psycho vent

I asked a very old man if he could give me any tips
on how to live a long life.
He said, "Just keep breathing as long as possible."

I went to a combination stress- and time-management
workshop. Now I worry much more efficiently.

My shrink said that if I didn't pay my bill,
he would let me go crazy.

My doctor is sure unlucky.
Every time I come in, he has an emergency
and I have to wait an hour and a half to see him.

NRA: No Real Assets.

If you are not going to use that brain stem,
give it to me.

psycho vent

I am at your disposal,
and your dishwasher isn't working so well either.

I hate housework. You sweep, mop, dust, make beds
and six months later, you gotta do it all again.

I actually saw an Oriental rug company
go out of business.

psycho vent

To the guy holding up the "Will Work For Food"
sign at 14th Street:
Funny, that's what I do.

Hope all of those people who got in my way last night
are happy; I missed "Star Trek."
I'm one ticked-off geek.

There is something I have to tell you:
You are the Vent, and I LOVE YOU, MAN!!!

psycho vent

I phoned my dad to tell him I stopped smoking
and he called me a quitter.

Just think, somewhere
"In the Heat of the Night" is on.

psycho vent

In synchronized swimming,
if one drowns do they all drown?
If they do, do they have synchronized lifeguards?

If a midget fortuneteller escaped from prison,
some nut would call the Vent and say,
"Small medium at large."

psycho vent

A wasp on my porch is acting very strange.
Do you think he has rabies?

When I called in a vent, instead of saying,
"Thanks for calling the Vent," the Vent voice said,
"You again?"

My wife told me to look at the vent
and now I'm stuck behind this dumb dryer.

I love this Vent thing.
It is the best thing in the paper. Of course,
that doesn't say much for the rest of the paper.

No matter the neighborhood of the Waffle House
you visit, there will be a guy with no shirt
standing at the pay phone next to his pickup,
which has a busted radiator.

Be safe on the Fourth.
Don't buy a fifth on the third.

I am so glad Fox has finally made a show for models.

Don't floss all your teeth.
Just the ones you want to keep.

psycho vent

Have you noticed that people getting out of the cars
with dark-tinted windows are always ugly?

I'm an old man, and I wonder why I never see
any caskets being given away on any TV prize shows.

People take an instant dislike to me
because it saves time.

To the nice venter who said Larry reads the Vent every day: Just wanted you to know that Curly reads it, too. And Moe writes it.

I don't think we need pay toilets downtown. The doorways and sidewalks seem to be working just fine.

Evangelists, clowns and armadillos simultaneously confuse and frighten me.

I've always found it easier to leave my house
through a window. I just found out the other day
I was born by Caesarean section.

If your cat comes to my bird feeder,
it will become dog food.

When the women with silicone breast implants
get their insurance settlements, do the guys
who paid for the implants get a rebate?

To the venter who wonders if you get a rebate
for paying for breast implants:
If you're still with the implantee, you get a rebate.
If you're not, you get nothing.

psycho vent

I wanted to go see "Apollo 13,"
but I'm not sure I'll understand it
because I haven't seen the other 12.

I hate it when they give you instructions
on how to hook up your VCR on videotape.

I'll work for food, but it has to be a candlelight dinner.

I have abandoned my search

for truth and I'm now looking

for a good fantasy.